On

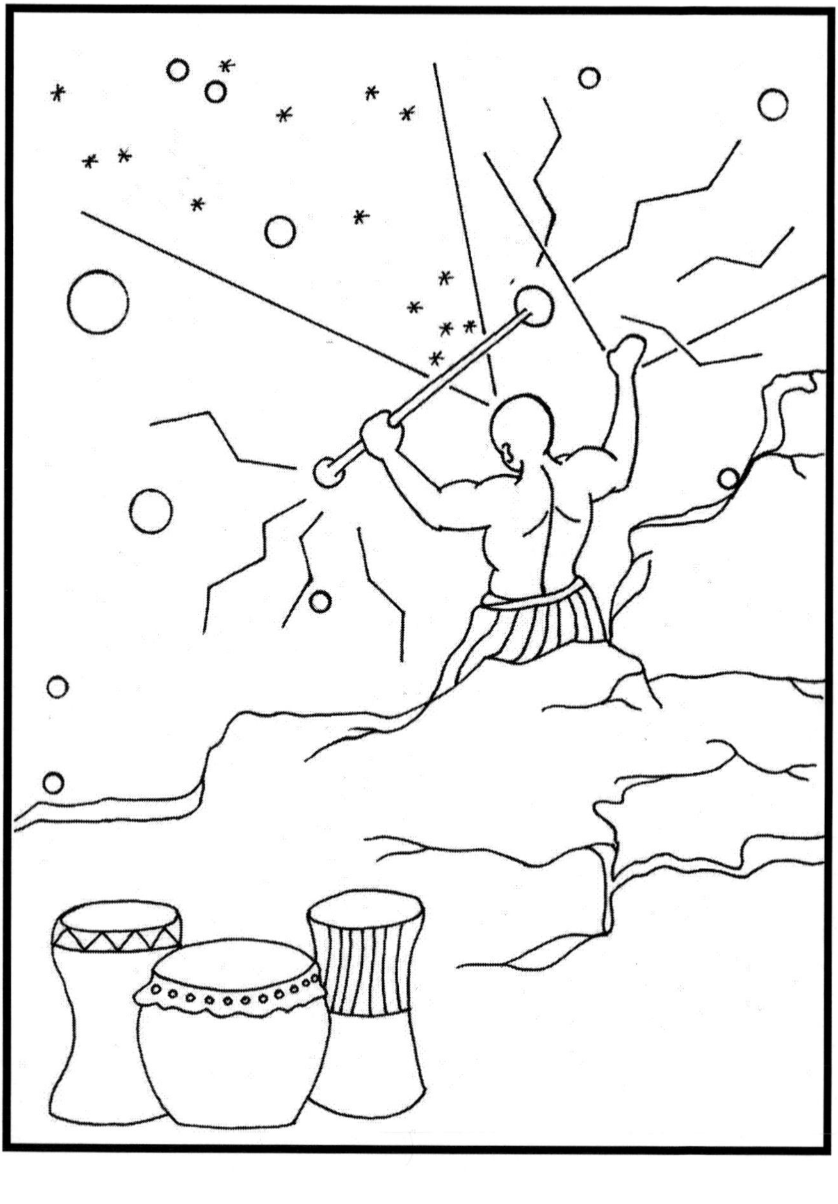

On

EXERCIRICLE
Keys to Museo-Ontology

On Mu Music Press

✹

New York

EXERCIRICLE

Keys to Museo-Ontology

Earth
Solar Cycle 3

Copyrighted © 2004

in the

United States of America

Library of Congress Control Number: 20-04096860

Last Edition

Illustrations by On

All Rights Reserved by Law

{No parts of these contents may be reproduced for monetary profit without the expressed written consent of the author}

Be Forewarned! The contents of this book are to serve solely for the good of humanity. Any conscientious violation of the intent of this purpose is highly impressive upon the karmic manifest.

File under:
Music-Ontology / Ontological Music-Physic Studies / Esoteric Music Science / Music Science / Esoteric Philosophy

*A very special 'thank you!' to
DJ Neva
for the
hours of contribution
to the design and layout of this book.*

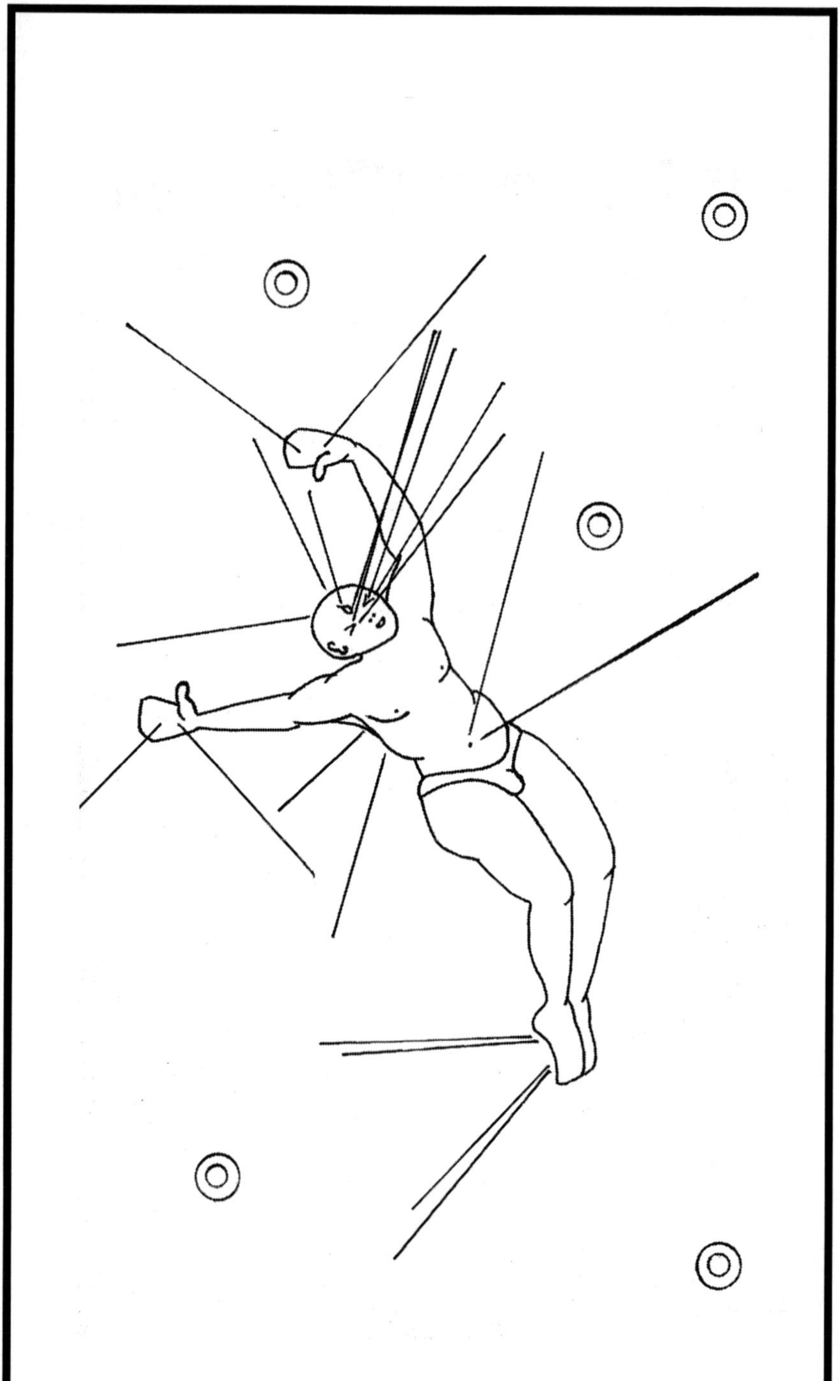

PREFACE
to the
Last Edition

This book that you are holding now pages the postulates of Ontological Music-Physics. The postulates are compiled of knowledge, enlightened experiences and intuition.

Contemplation in this book will induce a tangible reception on the wonder of the creative process. Inside may be found the seeds that continually bring forth one's inherited genius.

Keep this book and study from it often. Invariably, all who read from it will find a way to enter into the realms of their highest creative self.

For the Enlightenment of All Souls

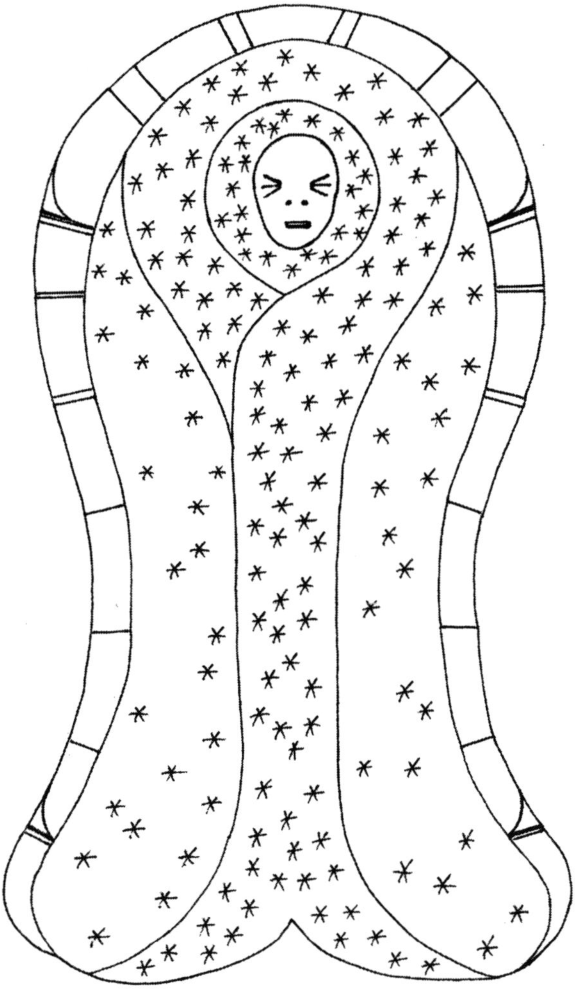

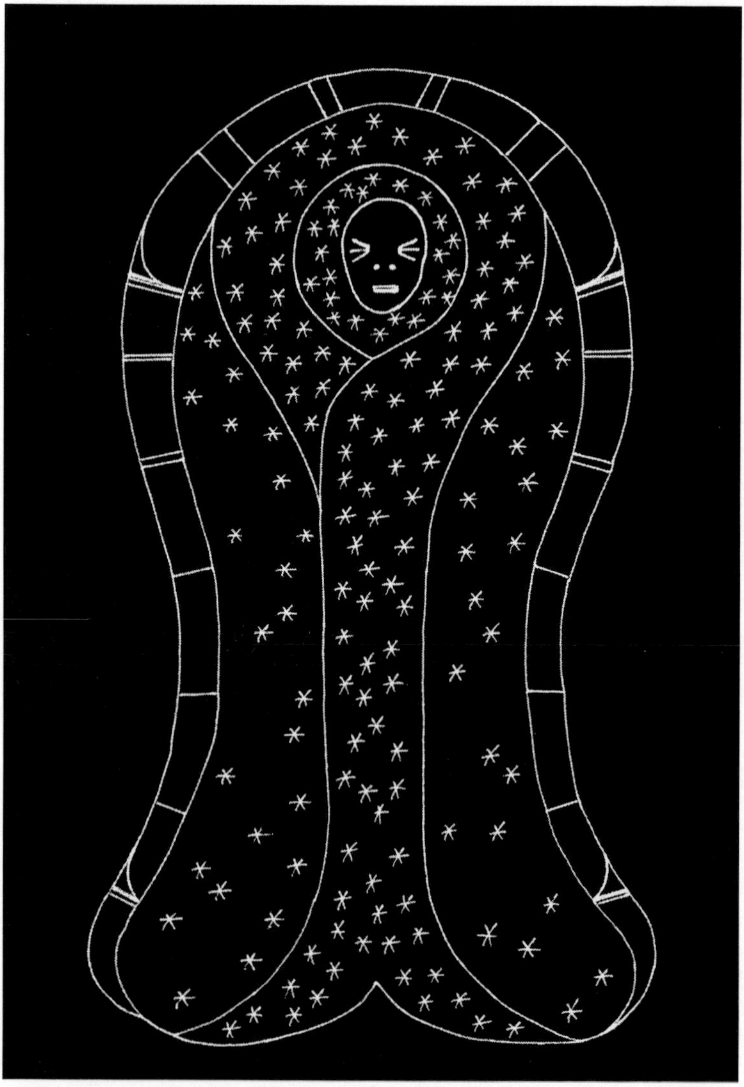

✻ ✻ ✻ ✻ ✻ ✻ ✻

All that Is, is the What of All.

****

All that Is, is of ever Creation.

All that Is, is ever Being.

****

All that Is, lets the wonders of its presence.

All that Is, lets the likeness of its Image(s).

All that Is, is ever becoming of something yet.

****

What Is, is in All that Is.

All that Is, is in What that All Is.

All of that What Is, is as It Is.

All Is that It Is.

****

Intelligence is inexplicable.

****

Intelligence permeates All that Is.

****

The current(s) of Existence(s) within All that Is, is pulse Intelligence.

****

Intelligence will light Intuition by Its presence.

****

Intuition is the innocence impression of Intelligence.

****

Intelligence lets Intuition into the Divine Mind of Cosmic Consciousness.

****

Intuition is suspended in Divine Mind.

****

Intuition lights the Spirit-Mind.

****

Intelligence lets the experience of Spirit-Mind act as the encoding for the impression(s) of (an) original cause.

****

Spirit-Mind lets the vibratory Universal Mind of God-Consciousness.

****

Spirit-Mind impression(s) light the experience of Being within Cosmic Consciousness.

****

Intuitive Spirit-Mind is free of Conscious-Being presence.

****

Intelligent Being permeates All that Is.

****

Intelligent Being exist as ever genesis Creation.

****

Intuitive knowledge of the Hu origin of Being is encoded within the Cosmic Consciousness.

****

Spirit-Intelligence illuminates Spirit-Mind Being throughout All that Is.

Spirit-Intelligence conducts Spirit-Mind Being into the dimension of Light.

Spirit-Intelligence lights Spirit-Mind Being upon the Act.

****

Mind lets Spirit-Consciousness throughout All that Is.

Mind lets Spirit-Consciousness into the dimension of Light.

Mind lets the Light of Spirit-Consciousness upon the Act.

****

Mind lets Spirit-Consciousness upon the vibratory-resonance of the Cosmos.

****

Intelligence begets (the) original Cause.

The Cause begets as residue (an) Impression(s).

Impression(s) beget Spirit-Mind Being.

Spirit-Mind Being lets Cosmic Consciousness.

Cosmic Consciousness lets Revelation.

Revelation will let the Reflection of Thought.

Reflection will induce Conception.

Conception begets the Cause-Idea.

The Cause-Idea begets the Act.

****

Mind in perfect repose reflects as imitation to the Act of original Creation.

****

Desire Spirit acted upon the Creative Will expresses (the) (a) Realiti(es) of Mind.

****

Intelligence conducts Mind to the experience of thought.

****

Thought(s) (is) (are) conducted to the Intelligence of All that Is.

****

Mind lights upon both the intelligent and unintelligible impression(s) of (a) thought(s).

****

Wonder thought is likened to the perfect attainment of all knowledge.

****

(An) Experience is the osmosis of Mind into the wonder of All that Is.

◆ ◆ ◆ ◆ ◆ ◆ ◆

✻ ✻ ✻ ✻ ✻ ✻ ✻

The vastness of the Darkness is original-reality.

****

Intelligence-radiance fuses Light as phenomenon.

****

The radiance of Light is phenomenal.

****

Light unveils the Omniverse.

****

Light conducts the inter-transcendence of Intelligence within the sphere(s) of the Omniverse.

****

Light is the firmament of All dimensions.

****

Dimension(s) within the Omniverse (is) (are) space(d) as (an) Eterntial(s).

****

Dimension(s) within the Omniverse (is) (are) space(d) by the expansion(s) of Infinite knowledge.

****

Intelligence-radiance permeates Space.

****

Space is of (a) (the) dimension of all Space-World-realiti(es).

****

Space is formal non-dimension.

******

Space alludes for a place of the pulse(s) of thought(s).

****

Space alludes for a place to measure distance(s) of projected thought(s).

****

Time Is as (an) illusion to (a) charted Space.

****

The Space-realiti(es) of Time exist only within the Space(s) of mental-perceptive Creative-realiti(es).

****

Intelligence-radiance lights the perceptive Creative-realiti(es) within (a) (the) flash(es) of (a) mental anticipation(s) in-between the passage(s) of time.

****

Time suggests the pulse(s) of mental-anticipation.

****

Mental anticipation is the inertial effect to seeking intelligent axis.

****

Time is relative to the power of perceptive thought-vibration(s) received of an object-receptive source that causes for (the) projection(s) of (a) (other) thought(s).

****

Time is relative to the number of perceptive thought-vibration(s) received of an object-receptive source that causes for (the) vibrational bodi(es).

****

The measured distance of (a) projected thought alludes to (a) (the) measurement(s) of time.

****

The distance(s) between (a) thought(s) is suspended in time.

****

Intelligence impression(s) of the motion(s) within time that allow for (one) creative thought to arrive at another creative thought will define what (a) distance is.

****

The distance in Space between two separate(d) realiti(es) in space represents the space(s) of the distance(s) between two separate(d) thoughts.

****

(A) distance traveled in Space is recognized when the Mind is receptive of the appearance(s) of at least two separate(d) expression(s) of creative causes.

****

The awakened Mind is able to perceive distance(s) in Space(s) by the Spatial-position(s) of (a) Creative-realiti(es).

****

(A) distance in Space will allude to the space(s) of potential thought projection(s).

****

(A) distance in Space will allude to the potential space(s) of thought projection(s).

****

The distance(s) projected by (a) thought-form(s) depend(s) upon the power, definition and clarity of (an) (the) original idea.

****

(A) Void is (as) in unreal Space.

****

(A) Void exists only as it is known by Intuition.

****

Void can not be realized.

****

(A) Void can not be known.

****

Unreal Space(s) is (are) in Void.

****

Void is (a) non-existent in (the) Space(s) of (the) vibrational-realiti(es).

****

Void opposes matter.

****

Void is anti-matter in Space, with only the potential to vibrate.

****

(A) Void is without (an) image.

****

Void can be experienced.

◆ ◆ ◆ ◆ ◆ ◆ ◆

✷ ✷ ✷ ✷ ✷ ✷ ✷

Intelligence forms the Creative-realiti(es) as designs of patterned Images.

****

All that Is appears as infinite pattern(s) of image(s).

****

The manifest form of a(n) image(s) is (are) also (the) anticipation image(s) to (a) formless of the Void.

****

An image is a composition of (a) patterned Creative-realiti(es).

****

(The) variant perceptive view(s) of (the) (an) image(s) are reflection(s) of (the) vibration(s) of (the) infinite-expanding Divine Will.

****

There exist infinite imagination beyond (an) (the) image(s).

****

Unknown images to the Mind have been secreted within All that Is.

****

The image(s) realized of Mind into the material world are expressions of the psyche tempo(s) of individual personaliti(es).

****

The image(s) realized of Mind into the material world are expressions of the psyche tempo(s) of grouped personaliti(es).

****

The image(s) realized of Mind into the material world are expressions of the contemplation and of the practices of (the) initiate(s).

****

The total of the experience(s) of (a) realiti(es) will not exhaust the potential(s) of the Image(s) of the Infinity that Is within All.

****

Mind can imagine whatever there Is.

◆ ◆ ◆ ◆ ◆ ◆ ◆

✹ ✹ ✹ ✹ ✹ ✹ ✹

Light upon Mind will reveal the Worlds upon Worlds.

****

A World is an embodiment of (an) electriciti(es) charged with resonating Intelligence patterns that simultaneously fuse together and separate, appearing images of Cosmic creation.

****

The forming of the Worlds is of the abstract cohesive force(s) of intelligence-attraction and intelligence-composite, created within the radiance of light and the reverberation of sound-substance.

****

All sides of the Divine World(s) exist before one another.

****

The elements of the Omniverse are attracted from Space by their likeness and by their representation.

****

All things of the World(s) have attained an influence upon one another.

****

The Cause-Idea induce(s) the activiti(es) of Creation within (the) space(s) of the World-realiti(es).

****

Magnetism is the expression of Intelligence in cohesion with itself.

****

Magnetism conducts the flow of the Desire Spirit within the Divine Will.

****

Magnetism becomes the current for vibration(s) of Intelligence that both attract and repel Desire Spirits.

****

Vibration is magnetism as current(s) of Intelligence.

****

Vibration is magnetism as Creative-reality.

****

Vibration(s) become(s) the energi(es) of (a) realiti(es).

****

Vibration(s) appear(s) as the motion(s) of realiti(es).

****

Realiti(es) is (are) the presence(s) of vibration(s).

****

Every reality will have an encoded vibration.

****

Vibration(s) is (are) the activiti(es) of (a) resonant-realiti(es).

****

Mediums are composites of vibration(s).

****

Gravity is the energy-reality of vibrational magnetism.

****

Gravity appears as in duality revealing the pairing of the risen and the fallen.

****

The dissipation(s) of energi(es) represent(s) the action(s) of gravity upon the crystallized state(s) of realiti(es).

****

Dissipation is the gravitational reaction to crystallization.

◆ ◆ ◆ ◆ ◆ ◆ ◆

✸ ✸ ✸ ✸ ✸ ✸ ✸

The Omniversal-sphere exhibits the perfect balance of All that Is as complete and separate Space-realiti(es) and are paired as such in opposition(s).

****

The Omniverse is balanced by the opposition(s) of separated Space-realiti(es).

****

The perceptive awareness of (the) entireti(es) is resulted from the transcended motion(s) of Space-World-realiti(es) that have permeated the receptive Mind.

****

(A) structural balance is achieved conceptually by the concentration to focus equally on real and abstract substances with intention to view each element complete to itself, yet also being dependent upon the whole expression.

****

Within the Acts of creation, a sense of balance is achieved by the kept awareness of the (perceived) entirety.

****

What is properly centered is also properly balanced.

****

(A) completeness comes from the fusion of oppositions.

****

Positioning presupposes (a) condition.

****

Only the subjugated is measurable.

****

Two similar existences will tend to share the same identiti(es), and will therefore fuse together.

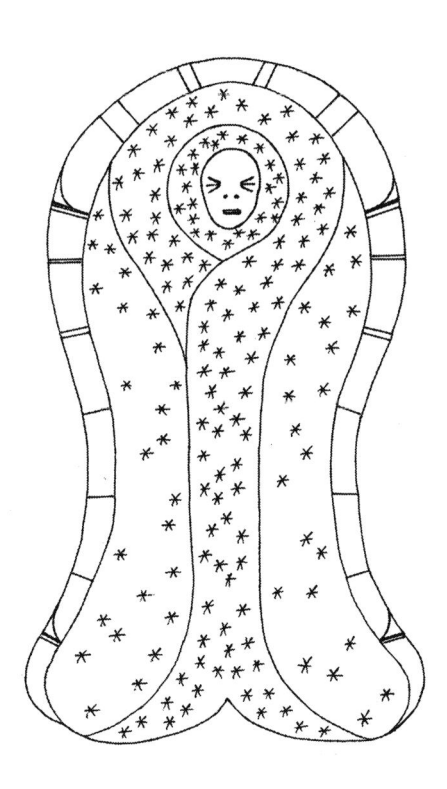

◆   ◆   ◆   ◆   ◆   ◆   ◆

✸ ✸ ✸ ✸ ✸ ✸ ✸

Mind encodes the ordering scheme of vibrational force(s) and (its) (the) resultant identiti(es) of (a) force field(s).

****

(An) Order(s) suggest the potential(s) to code-define what Infinity Is.

****

Order exhibits the patterned possibiliti(es) of (a) potential appearance(s) of (a) Space-World-realiti(es).

****

Order is a pattern of (a) World-realiti(es).

****

Order results from the transcendence of creative energi(es) as (a) posture(s) of complete composition(s).

****

What has been set in (an) order will start motion.

****

The relationship(s) of order(s) to Mind lights chaos.

****

Chaos is void of Act.

****

Chaos is void of Creative-realiti(es).

****

Chaos is void of Creative-order(s).

****

Chaos is an agitated state of existence.

****

Chaos is the reflection of (the) vibrational-realiti(es) as sympathetic dis-chordance.

****

Chaos and dis-order(s) may be trued by the magnetic vibration(s) of the Desire Will.

****

The Mind knows wisdom as truth or non-truth by the integrated positioning of the relationship(s) of (a) thought(s) within the pattern(s) of chaos and order.

****

The balance(s) between order(s) and chaos appear in the motion(s) of Space-World-realiti(es) in the instance(s) of the Act(s) of creative fusion(s).

****

The constant motion of transcending spaces of realiti(es) force order(s) to emerge from chaos.

****

Orders and chaos are conditions that weigh the state(s) of Being(s).

****

Orders and chaos are conditions that weigh the state(s) of (the) Spirit(s).

♦ ♦ ♦ ♦ ♦ ♦ ♦

All that appears will be of (its own) description as expression(s) of Intelligence.

****

All that appears is of the Cause-idea of the Divine Mind.

****

All that appears (will) correspond(s) to thought and creative desire.

****

All that appears will be of its own description by the make up of its existence.

****

All that appears will be of its own description by the degree of Intelligence reciprocity.

****

All that appears will be of its own description by the quality of its radiance.

****

All that appears will be of its own description by the quality of its resonance.

****

All that appears will be of its own description by the design of its form.

****

The image appearance of order emerging from chaos is the spiral.

****

The image appearance of chaos merging to order is (upon) the plane.

****

Motion(s) between the spaces of realiti(es) implies experience.

****

Experience between experience(s) implies (a) motion.

****

The image of the constant motion(s) of realiti(es) appear(s) as (the) (a) spin.

****

The motion(s) (within) (of) (the) (a) spin(s) (is) (are) symbolic to the image(s) of Infiniti(es).

****

The structure of the sphere is unto like the posture of infinite knowledge.

****

The formation(s) of the World(s) exists of Mind.

****

A form revealed into the World is the image of the progenitive Desire Mind.

****

The manifest physical form is expressed first as a design from within the Mind.

****

Form is spacial dimension.

****

A form is the cohesion of Space-World image(s).

****

The composition of (a) form is (also) the (a) (realized) design of (a) fused Space-World image(s).

****

A form is an image of (a) transcended space(s) of realiti(es).

****

The form exhibits the creation(s) from transcended space(s) of realiti(es).

****

The form exhibits the creation(s) of (a) manifest realiti(es).

****

What Is of All That Is ever radiates beauty.

****

What Is of All That Is retains and radiates beauty.

****

The beautiful is the lattice of proportions and relationships that mediate orders and chaos.

****

A beautiful form will balance (the) order(s) against chaos.

****

A beautiful form will balance (the) order(s) against chaos while engorging the physical senses.

****

A beautiful form will balance (the) order(s) against chaos while causing for the enlightenment of Mind.

****

The formless represent(s) a(n) image(s) not fused into a creation of (a) manifest realiti(es).

****

The formless (is) (are) a(n) imaged energi(es) without potential to morphortise.

❖ ❖ ❖ ❖ ❖ ❖ ❖

✸ ✸ ✸ ✸ ✸ ✸ ✸

All That Is, is upon the configuration(s) of pairs of expanding energi(es).

****

The sphere is as the image of expanding energi(es).

****

The Omniverse moves with sensitiviti(es) to the respect of energi(es).

****

Energi(es) throughout the Omniverse exist in infinite motion.

****

Energi(es) transcend(s) matter(s) as rhythmic pulsation that exhibit(s) varying degrees of power.

****

All energy will change after experiencing movement(s) from one dimension in space to another.

****

(A) change(s) in the composite(s) of (an) energi(es) will effect its qualiti(es).

****

Energi(es) existing within centripetal motion become(s) static-existent.

****

Energi(es) existing within centrifugal motion become(s) free-existent.

****

The fusion of oppositions releases energy.

****

The sphere is as symbol to expanding energi(es).

****

Explosive power is created by the interference of dis-chordant energy fields by crossing continuant energy fields.

****

The power of an explosion exhibits the intensity of crossing energy fields.

****

The degree(s) of an energy-mass are measurable by equation to the reciprocity of the duration of the force(s) of the causal effect(s) against the resistance of Chaos.

◆ ◆ ◆ ◆ ◆ ◆ ◆

✻ ✻ ✻ ✻ ✻ ✻ ✻

Thought(s) define the Mind experience(s) of (an) activi(es) within (a) space(s).

****

(A) thought(s) that appear(s) into the Space-World-realiti(es) (is) (are) (a) reflection(s) of Mind Will.

****

Thought identifies the image of the Desire Spirit.

****

Thoughts evolve within the constant movement(s) of perception(s) between the real and the abstract sphere(s) of Mind.

****

Thought moves (between) the conscious-realiti(es) of Mind.

****

The movement(s) of thought(s) light(s) the action(s) of spontaneous activiti(es) exchanged between Mind and Acts of Creation.

****

Thought exists as both positive and negative Mind.

****

(A) thought(s) that (is) (are) within the space(s) of a void can only be recognized by the let of intuition.

****

Logical thought results as the mental-desire is in accord to the Divine Spirit of the Infinite creation.

****

Thought is reflective response of the soul against World-realiti(es).

****

(A) thought-image(s) (is) (are) (a) reflection(s) of soul-energi(es).

****

The intensity of the rhythmic pulse of (a) thought-image(s) express(es) the depth of the power(s) of soul.

****

The various rates of speed(s) and qualiti(es) of (an) evolution(s) of thought development(s) will reveal the state(s) of (a) soul(s).

****

Thought projection(s) from one dimension of (a) space to another dimension of (a) space causes for the mental conceptualization of (a) Spiritual transcendence.

****

The speed(s) of (a) thought-projection(s) travelling through (a) space is calculated in accordance to the faciliti(es) of control that the Spirit commands over (an) act(s) of (the) creative manifest.

****

The degree(s) of the obscurity of (a) mental-receptive distance between one thought vibration to the next thought vibration defines what is the speed of (a) thought-projection.

****

The speed of (a) thought-projection in space is calculated in accordance to the facility of control that the Mind presents over a singular conception.

****

The rate(s) of (a) (the) mental reception(s) of (a) distance(s) in space between (a) thought vibrational-realiti(es) to (an)other thought vibrational-realiti(es) define(s) what the rate(s) of (a) (the) speed(s) of (a) thought-projection(s) is.

****

Thought(s) within and/or out of the space(s) of (a) manifest realiti(es) (is) (are) enacted by the physical bodi(es).

****

(A) thought form(s) (is) (are) (an) image(s) of (a) vibrational-realiti(es) transformed as Intelligent exchange(s) within the Mind.

****

The movement(s) of the Omniverse agitate (a) thought-form(s).

****

The qualiti(es) of (a) thought-form(s) and the abiliti(es) of (a) thought-form(s) to produce into the physical-realiti(es) a spiritual cause is reflective of the qualiti(es) and original power of the cause for spiritual love.

****

The qualiti(es) and depth(s) of (an) expressed thought-form(s) (is) (are) defined by the rate(s) of conceptualized finaliti(es) of (an) expression(s) of (a) thought-realiti(es) to the extent of the integration of realized world-realiti(es).

****

A thought-form is strengthened by the diligent exercising of (a) (that) thought-form.

****

A thought process is strengthened by the diligent exercising of (a) (that) thought process.

****

Mental concentration upon separate(d) thought-images will suggest intuitively a distance of space between forces of thought-vibration(s).

****

Mental concentration upon separate(d) thought-images will suggest intuitively a distance of space between forces of attracted thought-vibration(s).

****

Mental concentration upon separate(d) thought-image(s) will suggest intuitively a distance of Space between forces of distracted thought-vibration(s).

****

Concentration results from the willed effort to become aware of the spiritualized senses at the moment of the conscious waking upon the affect of a singular perception.

****

Concentration liberates the Mind of the bondage of the lower planes of existence.

****

The knowledge of a singular idea light upon cycles, forc(es) and the whole of the Spiritual affect.

◆ ◆ ◆ ◆ ◆ ◆ ◆

✴ ✴ ✴ ✴ ✴ ✴ ✴

Intelligence transforms into electra-magnetism by resonating against the frequenci(es) of attracting Desire Spirits, and as, will create physical bodies.

****

Intelligence transforms into electra-radiance by resonating against (the) physical bodi(es), and as, will light the reciprocating atmosphere(s) of both active and the passive life-force(s).

****

Electra-radiation and electra-magnetism exist as energi(es) within a matrix of opposite poles, and when fused together, make(s) up the force field(s) vital for the creation of Cosmic-substance.

****

Electra-radiation and electra-magnetism spontaneously and continually exchange themselves without end, causing for their explosive equal exchanges of power and of energi(es) at precise moments, thereby defining the potentialities of Cosmic creation.

****

Sound is the Image impression of Cosmic creation.

****

The appearance of sound is a wonder.

****

All that Is particles Sound.

****

Infinity particles into sound.

****

Sound particles what Infinity Is.

****

Sound particles exist in space as energi(es) responding in reaction to the electra-magnetic exchanges of elemental properti(es) of matter, experiencing immediate and constant crystallization(s) of sound-vibration(s).

****

Sound exists within (a) dimension(s) of itself.

****

Sounds exist within (a) dimension(s) of themselves.

****

Sound creates dimension(s).

****

Sound is the cohesive field(s) of (a) realiti(es).

****

Sound expresses (a) (the) world-realiti(es) of Infinity.

****

Sound expresses the fused energi(es) of Infinity.

****

World-realiti(es) (is) (are) as (the) firmament(s) to real-existence.

****

Real-existence is Lighted sound.

****

Energy is fielded as sound resonation.

****

Energy is fielded within sound resonation.

****

Energy is fielded about sound resonation.

****

A single sound represents a relationship to the infinite sound(s) of the Omniverse.

****

A single sound represents the infinite relationship(s) to the eternal vibration(s) of sound-energi(es).

****

Thought is carried within the motion(s) of (a) constructed sound-image(s).

****

Thought may be carried through sound-realiti(es).

****

Thought is carried within (a) crystallized sound-realiti(es).

****

The manifested thought form of the Desire Mind will crystallize as sound energy.

****

Light-radiance will cause the cohesion of electra-radiation to become present as sound energi(es).

****

Light-radiance as the cohesion of sound-energy becomes (a) (the) sonic form of (a) (the) resonate physical bodi(es).

****

The cohesion of electra-magnetism will cause for sound-energy to become materialized as a form of solid matter.

****

Sound as Intelligence transforms into electra-magnetism by resonating against the frequenci(es) of attracting Desire Spirits, and as, will create physical bodies.

****

Sound as Intelligence transforms into electra-radiance by resonating against (the) physical bodi(es), and as, will light the reciprocating atmosphere(s) of both active and the passive life-force(s).

****

Sound is the vibrational energy that crystallizes Life.

****

The presence of an existence corresponds to a design of patterned crystallized sound energi(es).

****

The appearance of the spirit of a being corresponds to a design of patterned crystallized sound-energies.

****

Sound-energi(es) is (are) crystallized composites of sound-vibration(s) drawn together by the gravity of like existence at immediate speed and disperse also at immediate speed, constantly.

****

Sound-energi(es) integrate(s) every space of reality within All that Is.

****

Sound-energi(es) pattern(s) (the) images of All that Is.

****

Sound-energi(es) will mirror patterns and images that express (a) posture(s) of Cosmic creation.

****

Sound-energi(es) (is) (are) bounded within the space(s) of realiti(es).

****

Sound-energi(es) (is) (are) illusion(s) to an (the) image(s) of resonate-realiti(es).

****

Sound-energi(es) will infuse the inaudible and the invisible World(s) of realiti(es).

****

The constant movement(s) of the Worlds account for the changes of vibration(s) within (the) sound-realiti(es) and consequently the expressed sound-energi(es) that reflect (the) order(s) of (a) (the) resultant manifest.

****

Sound-energi(es) will change form(s) after experiencing movement(s) between one dimension in space to another.

****

Sound-energi(es) will change character(s) after experiencing movement(s) between one dimension in space to another.

****

The qualiti(es) of (a) sound-realiti(es) is (are) determined by the influence(s) of the proximity of contrasting sound-energi(es) vibration(s).

****

Changes in the quality of (a) sound-realiti(es) will force the change(s) of (a) condition(s).

****

Sound-energi(es) in isolation will identify a measurable motion.

****

Sound-energi(es) identifi(es) (a) motion(s) of (a) realiti(es) according to the degree(s) of resonate feedback emitted from the subjected object.

****

The rhythmic movement(s) of crystallized sound-energi(es) will form the designs of matter.

****

Sound-energi(es) induce(s) the movement(s) of (a) (the) physical form(s) by the power of its pulse-impression(s) upon its matter.

****

The chang(es) of (a) physical form(s) exhibit(s) proof of (a) sound-energi(es) moving between (a) (its) realiti(es).

****

Sound-energi(es) impress(es) upon the state(s) of (the) physical-realiti(es).

****

Sound-energi(es) correspond to the state(s) of a (the) physical-realiti(es).

****

Sound-energi(es) reflect the state(s) of a (the) physical-realiti(es).

****

Sound-energi(es) refract the state(s) of a (the) physical-realiti(es).

****

Sound-energi(es) express the state(s) of (the) physical-realiti(es).

****

Sound-energi(es) give(s) definition to the state(s) of (the) physical-realiti(es).

****

Sound-energi(es) will cause effect(s) upon (the) physical bodi(es).

****

Separate sound-energies that vibrate the same in power and in time will fuse together, pre-supposing for (the) (resultant) implosion(s) and explosion(s) of (a) mass(es).

****

Sound-energi(es) as (a) directed force(s) upon an object that equals the mass weight of its vibrational density will distort both itself and the object of focus.

****

Sound-energi(es) may assume the character and make-up as an electricity.

****

Sound-energi(es) may assume the character and make-up of electrical energi(es).

****

Sound-energi(es) in motion will cause for the manifest of its vibration(s).

****

The power and force of (the) (a) sound manifest is known by to what degree sound-vibrations have impressed upon the immediate realms of the ethereal existence.

****

The vibrations of sound will define the physical world(s).

****

Sound vibrations within the space(s) of (the) immeasurable realiti(es) (is) (are) the attunator(s) for all beings of the world(s).

****

Sound-vibration(s) equaling the degree(s) of vibration(s) of (an) expanding mass-energi(es) will explode the force(s) of (a) contracting mass-energi(es).

****

Vibrational sound-energi(es), potential in free-space or in (a) defined-space realiti(es), will pulse in correspondence to (the) different potential rate(s) of (a) presence of Intelligence.

****

Vibrational sound-energi(es), potential in free-space or in (a) defined-space realiti(es), will pulse uniformly in correspondence to (the) different potential rate(s) of (a) receptive matter.

****

Sound-vibration(s) (will) pre-suppose(s) the void-vibration(s) that pre-suppose(s) silence.

****

Sound(s) and silence exist apart, thereby expressing two separate spheres of space.

****

Sound(s) and silence transcend each other while existing apart as two separate spheres of space.

****

Silence is not receptive to sound-energi(es).

****

Silence expresses the potential of (a) vibratory sound-energi(es) that (is) (are) not aligned to tune the physical bodies.

****

Silence is the illusion to (a) physical appearance(s).

****

Physical dis-appearance(s) is (are) the illusion(s) of dissipated sound-energi(es).

****

Sound is the illusion to silence.

****

Silence pre-supposes sound.

****

Sound proves silence.

****

The space of the clair-aural exchanges the Intelligence of (the) resonating/non-resonating, vibratory/non-vibratory sound-silence realiti(es).

****

Sound-Silent realiti(es) define(s) the space(s) of clair-aural.

****

Sound-Silent realiti(es) prove(s) the world of clair-aural.

****

Noise is sound-energy that exist as an unintelligible reality.

****

Noise reflects the presence of sound-energi(es) that are unable to exchange Intelligence to the physical senses.

****

Noise exists between realiti(es) and (the) (a) void.

****

Noise is the sound-energy of chaos.

****

Noise is the sound-vibrational manifest of chaos.

****

Noise is the sound-reality of chaos.

****

The power of sound opens the transcendental communication(s) between realiti(es).

****

The power of sound opens the transport-expressway(s) between realiti(es).

****

The manipulation of sound-science can create vibra-beings of greater potential than our selves.

◆ ◆ ◆ ◆ ◆ ◆ ◆

✳ ✳ ✳ ✳ ✳ ✳ ✳

White Light is the visual appearance of the total of vibratory sound-energi(es) fused together.

****

White Light is the visual appearance of the Grande Scale.

******

Color expresses shades of Intelligence.

****

Color in the atmos sphere(s) represent(s) the Intelligent separation of the qualiti(es) of sound-energi(es).

****

Color in the atmos sphere(s) becomes the visual appearance of segmented sound-energi(es).

****

Spectra science will give insight(s) into the explanation(s) of sound-energy composite(s).

****

Music is symbolic to the (a) realization of sound as color.

****

The Mystic Scale arises from, extends to and returns to the paired sound-silence reality-sphere(s).

****

The sound-energy vibration(s) of the rising musical scale represent(s) the creative motion of fusing energy-vibration(s) that manifest the images and forms within All.

****

The sound-energy vibration(s) of the rising musical scale is (are) the aural vibratory realiti(es) of the luminous-realiti(es) found within broken white light.

****

The rising musical scale divided into seven tones within an 'octave' range pre-supposes the aural-vibrational realities as reflective of the seven-segmented luminous-vibratory realiti(es) found within white light.

****

A musical scale ordering accepts the pattern(s) of sound-impression(s) that seemingly best relate to the experience-sounds of the Omniverse.

****

Musical scales are representations of the approximations of space(s) between similar and dissimilar sound-tone energi(es).

****

A musical scale is a set order of sound-tones accepted (by) (as) a common psyche tempo of a culture-identity.

****

The relationship(s) of (a) sound-tone(s) within a formalized scale will become subject(s) to (the) (a) the listener's psycho-intuitive make-up as part of (the) (a) music(al) (performance).

****

The amplitude of sound represents to what degree (a) sound(s) will project its vibration.

****

The amplitude of sound represents its proximity to the physical sense.

****

The amplitude of sound represents to what degree sound has integrated a defined space.

****

Pitch represents a constant frequency of sound vibration(s) within a defined space.

****

Pitch(es) of sound(s) bewares the physical senses to the pulsation of sound-energi(es).

****

Pitch(es) of sound(s) bewares the physical senses to the separation(s) of sound and silence.

****

The (potential) capabiliti(es) of (a) sound-energi(es) to be absorbed into (a) receptive physical matter is represented by the variances between the space(s) of (a) pitch(es).

****

The differences between (a) pitch(es) represent(s) the potential abiliti(es) of a physical matter to be receptive to sound-energi(es).

◆ ◆ ◆ ◆ ◆ ◆ ◆

✺ ✺ ✺ ✺ ✺ ✺ ✺

A sense of musical dialect directs the use of musical material.

****

(A) musical dialect suggests an identity for the sense perceptions of (a) creative thought(s).

****

Compositional use of musical material(s) is symbolic to the ordering of sound energi(es) integrated into silence.

****

A musical tone is characterized by its quality of sound.

****

A musical tone is identified by the residual impression(s) from the intention(s) of (a) mind-realiti(es).

****

The conscious placement(s) of sound-tones exhibit the knowledge of Space as creative reality.

****

Lyricism exhibits the intellectual, instinctive and desire realms of consciousness.

****

Lyricism represents the depth and beauty of a spiritual awakening.

****

A lyrical succession of musical sound-tones will arrest the physical senses.

****

A lyrical succession of musical sound-tones will inspire (for) creative thought.

****

A lyrical succession of musical sound-tones will please the physical senses.

****

A lyrical arrangement of sound-tones will communicate expressions of reasoned thought(s) that reflect the respect of logical balances perceived of Nature.

****

A melody communicates a refined expression into the World-realiti(es).

****

The communication of a melody reflects the mental perception of the Life-sustaining sound-energies vital to the evolution of soul.

****

A consciously created melody becomes a tonal record of the creative process.

****

Creative evolution is expressed within the rhythm(s) of change(s) of perception, patterned of Mind from the rate(s) of successive contemplation(s) upon a completed (physical) image to the next completed (physical) image.

****

The perpetual rhythm of the Creation outlines the cycles of appearance, dis-appearance and re-appearance.

****

The codes of the World(s) are carried by the rhythmic pulses of the Cosmic Wind.

****

Cosmic Music moves in continuos cycles of rhythmic expansions and contraction.

****

Cosmic Music moves in the continual and simultaneous motion of oppositions, creating both centripetal and centrifugal forces in rhythmic synchronicity.

****

The motion(s) of Life exists as (a) rhythm(s) in the eternal movement(s) of the Omniverse.

****

The natural rhythm(s) in Life-cycle(s) order the essential motional experience(s) which give light to self-realization and Divine Knowledge.

****

The Mind recognizes the movements of Nature as ordered by the rhythm(s) of Life-experience.

****

Our Life-rhythm(s) become(s) the transcendental experience(s) of our evolution(s).

****

Experience changes of Life represent the motion(s) of Life-rhythm(s).

****

Rhythm exhibits the balance of Spirit against the activiti(es) of the Omniverse.

****

Rhythm is time divided within the pulsation of Universal activiti(es).

****

The patterned movements of (a) rhythm represent(s) the cyclic laws of Cosmic creation.

****

The rhythmic dimension(s) of music represent(s) awareness(es) to the ordering possibilities of energy pulsation.

****

Rhythm represents devotional acknowledgement.

****

The rhythmic movement(s) of expressive thought(s) induced by music appear(s) into the World as the physical dance.

****

The physical dance exhibits a control of the body against the rhythmic vibrations of the Omniverse.

****

The art(s) of music and dance express the balances of Cosmic harmony.

****

The self perfected in all-sidedness reflects the Divine harmony of the Universe.

****

The sounds of the Omniverse harmonize All, attuning our mental dispositions and patterns of expression.

****

Harmony represents the postures of sound-energies fused together.

****

The harmony of (a) relationship(s) should be understood as (a) posture(s) of fused sound-energi(es) that share in a defined space.

****

Profound harmonic expression(s) can arise from either simple or clustered posture(s) of sound-energi(es).

****

Harmony is recognized in Mind as being constant variation to the pulsation of logical thought.

****

Music will satisfy the soul when logical thought is in harmony to the Will of Divine Spirit.

****

Musical harmony will pattern the whole scheme of relationships found within all of the manifestations of the World(s).

****

The metamorphoses of (a) (the) spiritualized Being is the expansion of continual harmonic progressions.

******

Understand that the whole of the Universe is one vast musical instrument.

****

An instrument is only instrumental.

****

A musical instrument breathed into is symbolic to an extension of the Prahnic pulse of the Universe.

****

All musical instruments are percussive except for those that are breathed into.

****

Percussion and its effects are symbolic to the elements of physical nature and of the space(s) of the material World-reality.

◆ ◆ ◆ ◆ ◆ ◆ ◆

✷ ✷ ✷ ✷ ✷ ✷ ✷

The life-current of Creation moves through the aetheric seas and into the more dense physical senses.

****

The physical-manifest space of (a) realiti(es) is experienced by the physical senses.

****

The impressions of the Universe upon the physical senses define the tangible-physical realiti(es) of existence.

****

The creative Will tends to repress the limitations of the physical-capable realiti(es).

****

What (is) (are) (a) physical-realiti(es) (is) (are) also illusion(s) (of) (to) creative image(s).

****

The ether of Intelligence is transmitted through the physical senses.

****

About the Atma is fielded the Atmos of electric current of force(s) of Life.

****

The Prahna is a current field of both active and potential spirit-energi(es) that exist about the Atma.

****

The Prahna is a current field of both active and potential spirit-energi(es) that exist in (an) (the) Atma-sphere(s).

****

The Prahna is a current field for the transformation of spiritualized-energi(es) as creative intelligence(s) of which brings forth life into a Being.

****

The Atma of a Being purports the Life-force of that Being.

****

Light is attracted into the Atma as breath.

****

Energi(es) (is) (are) attracted into the Atma as breath.

****

(An) Impressionable(s) (is) (are) attracted into the Atma as breath.

****

Spirit(s) (is) (are) attracted into the Atma as breath.

****

The source(s) of spirit-magnetism (is) (are) carried in the Atma.

****

The Atma-sphere(s) of sound-energi(es) vitalize spirit.

****

Sound-energy is ghosted by the push of Atma from the spiritualized Being into the Atmos-sphere(s).

****

Sound-energy is alivened by the push of Atma from the spiritualized Being into the Atmos-sphere(s).

****

Sound-energy is vitalized by the push of Atma from the spiritualized Being into the Atmos-sphere(s).

****

Sound will carry thought within the electro-magnetic current(s) of Atma.

****

Atma purports the electric current(s) of spiritualized sound(s) as thought-radiance.

****

Atma purports the electric current(s) of spiritualized sound-voice(s) as thought-radiance.

****

Atma purports the electric current(s) of spiritualized sound-word(s) as thought-radiance.

****

The Prahna channels the way of (an) Intelligence-impressionable(s) upon the Being-Mind.

****

The current(s) of prahna-breath is (are) symbolic to the motions of the creative process.

****

A conscious use of prahna-breath will dispel countering force(s).

****

The rhythm of the prahna-breath pre-supposes the potential pattern(s) of a being's make-up.

****

The breath currents the sustenance fields of Life-waves.

****

The breath sustains the movement(s) of the physical-being bodi(es).

****

The manifest bodi(es) of (the) physical-realiti(es) (is) (are) (the) (an) image(s) of the absorption of Life-waves.

****

The rhythmic life-cycles of a being are seen patterned against the pulse(s) of the being's Atma-sphere(s).

****

The electra-magnetic energi(es) directed through a resonating voice will charge the physical being.

****

The electra-magnetic energi(es) directed through a resonating voice will change the physical being.

****

The electra-magnetic energi(es) directed through a resonating voice will charge physical mass(es).

****

The electra-magnetic energi(es) directed through a resonating voice will change physical mass(es).

****

The crystallized sound-vibration(s) of the voice beget(s) the definitive idea(s) of thought-meaning.

♦ ♦ ♦ ♦ ♦ ♦ ♦

✶ ✶ ✶ ✶ ✶ ✶ ✶

The voice carries the inner Life-force expressed of the Mind into the physical-reality.

****

The voice transmits power that can command the physical world(s).

****

The voice impresses the World(s) as an active force, measured in degrees of power, beauty and wisdom.

****

The voice impresses both the World of the physical-reality and the World of the inaudible-unseen.

****

Within the eyes is the window for the Light(s) of the soul; Within the voice is carried the sonic-essence of the soul.

****

One's quality of voice is as unique to a spirit as a soul is to a Being.

****

The voice mirrors the quality of spirit that is within the Being.

****

Within the voice is found the Life-force of the personality.

****

The forward or retracting motion of one's Life can be heard in the presence of one's voice.

****

The voice is a mirror of one's evolution, of one's character and of the age of one's wisdom.

****

Efforts to master the power of one's own voice will satisfy the inner spirit.

****

The art of self-mastery relies upon the willingness for one to want to listen.

****

Every living Being is created tuned according to their Cosmic correspondence.

****

The discovery of one's "key note" will liberate the dormant Spirit personality.

****

The inspirational personal voice is the testament upon the infinitely evolving music of the Cosmos from the source of All that Is.

****

The inspiritualized voice arises of the wisdom-vibrations of virgin Spirit(s).

****

Every word spoken and thought awakened will have its reciprocal impression in the psyche, and correspondingly in the Atmos-sphere(s).

****

Words and thoughts are constantly creating invisible atmosphere(s) about the Life.

****

Word-sound is the sound-vibration transference of Intelligence.

****

Word-sound(s) will fuse together the inner and the outer sides of Mind.

****

The Word is upon the Intelligence of ordered sound-power.

****

The power of the sound-word will cause all the life-experiences of this world to be described by a single revelation.

****

The unseen can be revealed by the power of sound-word vibration.

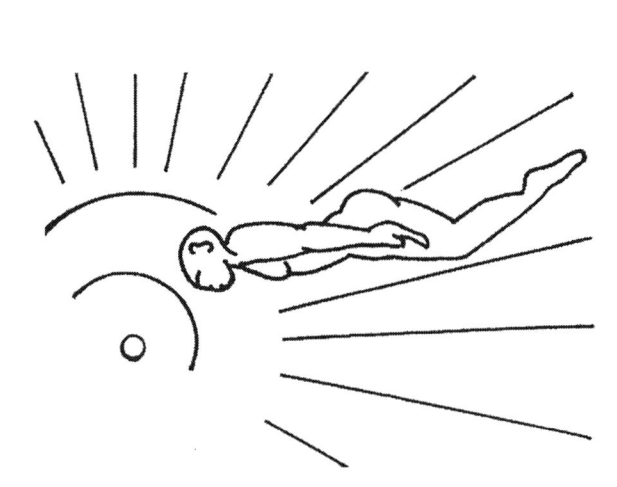

◆ ◆ ◆ ◆ ◆ ◆ ◆

✳ ✳ ✳ ✳ ✳ ✳ ✳

Higher Orders of Being live in Universality without peripherals, expressing the wonder of Spiritual transformation to every creature, and so tunes all consciousness to the enactment(s) of Creation.

****

The Higher Orders of Being are endowed with the powers to create whole worlds and to transform unseen worlds into the Atmos of an immediate reality.

****

The Higher Orders of Being see the appearances of Life about Intelligence and beauty before discerning to recognize any form of embodiment(s).

****

The Higher Orders of Being will recognize the composites of the Crystalline Lattice hidden within the Music of the Spheres.

****

The Higher Orders of Being recognize the weight of sound(s) in the Atmos and as the transferor(s) of Intelligent impression(s).

****

The Intelligence of creative energy will fuse the music(s) of the higher dimensions to Light and phenomenon.

****

Cosmic Music crystallizes the impressions of Life and codes the order(s) of vibration(s) that is the World.

****

The structure of a musical design is expressed by elements of the infinite facets of the Crystalline Lattice.

****

Music is designed thought projection that transmits the resonance of coded intelligence throughout the World(s).

****

The secreted codes within Creation is as one vast musical design.

****

Music illuminates Intelligence about the Desire Will, translating the code(s) of Divine Will to the consciousness of the receptive Being.

****

The Ontological scientist is the Divine Musician.

****

The Ontological scientist will express from the osmosis of Intelligence the transference of (the) creative Act.

****

The Ontological scientist will express from the osmosis of Intelligence the potential(s) of (a) spirit(s).

****

The High and enlightened musicians will posture themselves as likened to (a) conductor(s) of Cosmic consciousness, offering the world a spiritualized experience.

****

The enlightened musician seeks continual revelation into the potential(s) of the power of music.

****

Spiritualized music will awaken one's Intuitive conscious.

****

Music science will explain both the measurable and the immeasurable equations of (the) Universe(s).

****

Contemplation as Cosmic-harmonic pulse will perfect the conditions for creating (the) world-reality to compliment the Desire Spirit.

****

The science of music seeks to intellectualize an art of spirit-expression.

****

The science of music teaches the harmony of life against life.

****

The musician-scientist designs from the world(s) of vibratory resonance.

****

Music designed by intention to mirror the nature of things will also describe a mental reflection upon Creation.

****

Consciously created music forms designed within centripetal motion will have a diminishing effect upon its object.

****

Consciously created music forms designed within centrifugal motion will have a magnetic effect upon its object.

****

Repetition of musical materials using both ordered centripetal and centrifugal motions will have an inspirational effect upon the Intuitive Mind.

****

Earthly music presents itself in (a) (the) World-realiti(es) according to the proximity of the creative thought-projection against the vibratory elements of its make-up.

****

Earthly music that intends to express the codes of the Cosmos will mirror the music of the spheres.

****

The limitations of earthly music cause for the inability to describe what All Is.

****

Musical reality exist as an alignment of (a) vibration(s) that express(es) the thought designs of the creative consciousness.

****

Music should be understood as an outer-personal presence that appears Intelligence before disappearing unintelligible existence.

****

Cosmic music expresses the balance of space(s) between the elements in the motion(s) of the creative-manifest.

****

The appearance(s) of (the) (a) divine music(s) express(es) the at-one-ment to the motion(s) of the Cosmos.

****

Music is the patterned sound organizations of Intelligent Will.

****

Music is organized segmented sound.

****

Music is (the) (an) order of sound-energi(es) that encodes the physical bodi(es).

****

Music is (the) (an) order of sound-energi(es) that tune(s) the physical bodi(es).

****

Music is (the) (an) order of sound-energi(es) that de-tune(s) the physical bodi(es).

****

Music can encode both formal-dimensional space and non-dimensional space.

****

Music bridges unconsciousness to consciousness, the formless to the form.

****

Music of the here-now transmits the partials of music-past and music-future.

****

What appears to be new is arrived at from (a) (the) perceptive viewing of (a) (the) manifest-realiti(es) in an enlightened moment of Mind.

****

The acceptance and the longevity of a musical innovation is determined by to what degree it has harmonized against the developing (grouped) psychic disposition(s).

****

Profound changes of musical expression will effect the social-political environment of a society.

****

Music will facilitate the art of learning to concentrate and to discovery of the inner self.

****

Changes in one's sonorous correspondence will alter the spiritual condition.

****

The vibrations of one's self will cause for the music about one's whole being.

◆ ◆ ◆ ◆ ◆ ◆ ◆

✳ ✳ ✳ ✳ ✳ ✳ ✳

Intelligence Is, as radiance of Its pure essence, It that lights the Spirit(s) and dusts the Soul(s).

****

The illumination(s) of Divinity may be recognized as a manifest of a single sound-image that can not be described. Any description exists only from Intuition.

****

Cosmic creative movement will force change(s) of vibration(s) about the bodi(es) and will record in time and space the morphosis of Life.

****

Eternal Life exists. It is embraced within the current of the infinite Intelligence that permeates All that Is.

****

The force of Life is veiled within abstract meta-physic and real-physic designs.

****

The Life-ghost exists as a fusion of the sphere(s) of designed Life-realiti(es) with the Spirit-will.

****

The Life-ghost enters into Life as a wonder sound.

****

The Life-force of a Being is strengthened by the expansive potential to retain of the Intelligent radiation.

****

The Life force(s) of a Being diminish(es) when (it) (they) can not position (itself) (themselves) to be receptive of the Spirit-will.

****

Acts in the imitation of nature forces the Desire Spirit to know natural-reality as the experience-castor of life.

****

Life is as the material existence of sound diminishing to its perfect state.

****

Life force(s) diminish when void in chaos.

****

Continued dis-chordance pre-supposes the eventual resolve of a body state.

****

Death is defused Life-force.

****

A ghost is the Spirit experience entering into (an) original posture.

****

A ghost is the Spirit experience returning to (an) original posture.

****

(A) Spirit(s) rest within (the) creative energi(es) at pose in space before being willed by Divine Mind as a living experience.

****

The Spirit attributes its evolution to the experience(s) of (a) (the) activiti(es) of willed creative thought.

****

An awakened Spirit will give inner tranquility to the soul and the ability for the self to rightly view the Cosmos.

****

(The) Spirit(s) move(s) by expansion.

****

The evolving Spirit learns wisdom(s) upon time within space(s) as an experience that is ever expanding.

****

Spirit and Nature face one another, each beholding the other.

****

The Spirit reaches into the physical-world realit(es) through the physical senses.

****

Practices of Spiritual purification will tune the Being to the vibrational laws of the Universe.

****

The Spirit of (a) Divine Will in motion becomes the experience of the Soul.

****

The soul is the essence that conducts the experience-transcendence of (the) Divine creative image(s) into the world(s) of (the) appeared realiti(es).

****

The experience of the soul is not bound within the space(s) of (a) dimension(s).

****

The metamorphosis of (a) soul is induced by the affixation(s) of spirit-will upon the postures of Divine Design.

****

Development of soul is directly related to the inspiration potential of the Spirit-Being to absorb Divine Intelligence.

****

Development of soul responds directly to spiritualized involvement and receptive capacity to absorb the vibrations of Light and sound.

****

The power(s) of creative force(s) will enlighten the soul.

****

The enlightened soul becomes the lighted body.

****

The Light about the Being is the illumination of the quality of thought(s) and nature(s) within it's Atmos.

****

The Light about the Being is the illumination of the power of the Life-force within its Atmos.

****

The nature of a Being is as the Light of the Atmos about that Being.

****

Enlightenment will cause a Being to express love-desire and to seek its source.

****

Enlightenment will cause a Being to express the love-desire to attempt perfection of personality.

****

Enlightenment will cause a Being to express love-desire to want to hear the infinite dialects of Cosmic Music.

****

Enlightened embodiment is the abstract reality of eternal creation.

****

An enlightened body is eternally creative.

****

An enlightened body is at home in space.

****

An enlightened body is able to astral project at will.

****

Planetary Ascension is an activation of Lightbody.

****

Light will illume the Atmos. Mind will aethereate the Atmos. Sound will crystallize the Atmos.

◆ ◆ ◆ ◆ ◆ ◆ ◆

✳ ✳ ✳ ✳ ✳ ✳ ✳

The significance of any experience depends upon the love for that experience.

****

The potential(s) of (a) creative energi(es) (is) (are) increased as contrasting creative energi(es) are drawn together towards a creative image of Divine Will.

****

The spiritualized forc(es) of (a) Divine Will induced by a wisdom of love design the centering and the absolute purpose of (a) creative expression.

****

The Divine Will centers itself as absolute in the Cosmos when the Spirit is moved by the wisdom of love.

****

Love-wisdom is the gift of Intelligent impressions received of the Mind as the I moves within the flow of Spirit metamorphosis.

****

Love-wisdom is as knowing that Spirit Is, and is perfect upon Divine Will.

****

The Being responds to the relationships of love that offer a sense of purpose to the desire of the Spirit will.

****

True inspiration is a realization of beauty induced by wisdom and love.

****

Life within love is absolute existence.

****

The extensiveness of I-creativity permeates the Omniverse, knowing every star of imagination.

****

The extensiveness of I-creativity is self-realization within the realms of wisdom and love.

****

The proficiency of I-creativity depends upon the degree(s) of mastery of the acts that induce (the) creative process.

****

Use(s) of the act(s) perfected as a conscience pursuit towards the mastery of self will broaden the space(s) of I-creativity.

****

Consistency is the result of discipline.

****

Discipline the self in order to experience the most profound freedoms.

****

A discipline results as a concentration towards commanding to knowledge a singular idea.

****

Probable visions of the future result from the study of creative order(s).

****

The atmospheres of the self attest to the attainment of musical sensibilities.

****

The applied use of developed psychic power will awaken the conscious to higher creative capabilities.

****

Artistic mastery within the creative process is accomplished by the fusion of Spirit into the space(s) of the infinite Intelligence of Desire Mind.

****

Creative genius is recognized within the archetypal pattern(s) of the realized creative work.

****

If (a) (an) (creative) expression is (a) reflection of Mind, then there is (a) Spiritualized relationship of Being to the objectivity of Life.

****

Creative expression corresponds to the objectiviti(es) of the respect(s) of Life.

****

Changes of the personality will occur as a result of practiced contemplation upon What All Is.

****

To the human being, music is spiritual reflex.

****

To the human being, music is spiritual reflection.

****

To the human being, music is spiritual refuse.

****

Music will change (a) Karma.

****

Music from the depth of soul becomes expressed as the 'cry of love'.

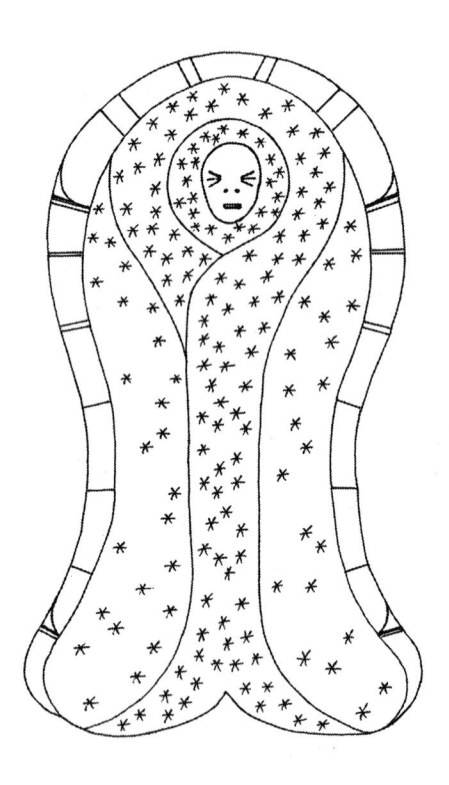

◆ ◆ ◆ ◆ ◆ ◆ ◆

The Planes of Real-Existence

Eternity	Infinity
Realm of Sounds	Realities
Realm of Forms	Possibilities
Realm of Numbers	Manifests
Realm of Lighted (Color) Impressions	Separations of Manifests
Realm of Music	Spaces of Creative Imaging
Realm of Freedom	World of Consciousness
Realm of Beauty and Perfection	Spiritualized Existence
Realm of Unlimited Possibilities	Cosmic Experienced
Realm of Atomic Invisibility	Absorption into Astral Light

The Seven Heavens

Heaven of Salvation

Heaven of Karma-Joy

Heaven of Love-Joy

Heaven of Love-Wisdom

Heaven of Enlightenment

Heaven of Creation

Heaven of Splendor

The Worlds of the Spirit(s)

(Grosser)
Meta-Physic Body
Mental Cloud
Soul Essence
Spirit-Mind Substance
(Adamic Dust / Evian Mist)
Spirit Innocence
In-Spiritualized Being
Light Body
(Finer)

The Activity of Being

Isolant Non-Active
Isolant-Active
Joined-Active
Joined Inter-Active { Independent Joined Inter-Active
{ Inter-Dependent Joined Inter-Active

Energy Polarity

Mental Plane: { He = (–) negative   Physical Plane: { He = (+) positive
{ S'he = (+) positive   { S'he = (–) negative

Environments of Real-Existent Bodies

<u>Omni-present</u>: { Astral Light – Cosmic-Radiance – Incandescent Gas }
<u>Vital Gases</u>: { Nitrogen – Hydrogen – Oxygen }
<u>Elemental</u>: { Fire (fluidal + terrestial) – Water (earth + fire) – Earth (igneous + aqueous) – Air }
<u>Chemical</u>: { Sulphur – Carbon – Nitric Acid – Salt – Ammonia (Salt of Amen) }
<u>Mineral</u>: { Iron – Tin – Lead – Copper – Gold – Silver – Mercury }

Atmospheres
{positive-spinning, negative-spinning, non-spinning (neutralized)}

Heat / Cold

Wet / Dry

Radiated { luminosity, illumination

Electrified { electro-radiance, electro-magnetism

Exploded / Imploded

Exposed / Insulated

Atomic charge spinning / Atomic charge non-spinning

Motions of the Elemental Properties of Real-Existent Bodies

<u>Fluidity</u> {osmotic motion}

<u>Gaseity</u> {aeroformic motion}

<u>Irradiation</u> {actinic motion}

<u>Dissolution</u> {vacuaic motion}

<u>Coagulation</u> {cohesive motion}

Nine Vital States of Force-Existence upon the Motions of Real-Existence

Gravity {magnetic-attractive}

Repellantcy {magnetic-repellant}

Levity {ethereal motion}

Celerity {voltaic motion}

Contraction {atrophic motion}

Expansion {hypertrophic motion}

Agitation {reactive motion}

Quiescence {cataleptic motion}

Paradigm Shift {inverted motion}

Word-sounds of Vital Postures of the Manifests of Creative Motion(s)
(from the alpha beta order of spoken symbols)

Arc (elliptic motion)	{ ark, a'ra'k(a), ark(a), arak }
Ray (helio motion)	{ ra, rai, ra I }
Wave (oscilli motion)	{ wa vah, w'ave, (y)a ve(h) }
Circle (concentric motion)	{ c' I ra' c'el, I'ra'el }
Spin (gyrostatic motion)	{ s'pi'(n), s'pi'I'(nu) }
Spiral (helico motion)	{ s'pi'ra'el, s'p'I'ra'el }
Pyramid (oblique motion)	{ pi'ra'mi' d(a), p'I'ra'm'I'(d), pi'ram'I (d) }
Sphere (omni motion)	{ s'fe'ra, s'p'he'ra, s'p(i)'he'ra }

The Planes of the Psyche

Realm of the Seven Senses

Physical	Mental
Sight	Desire
Hear	Resplendence
Smell	Instinctive
Taste	Sustaining
Touch	Abstract
Thought	Concrete
Intuition	Love-Wisdom

Physic Nature	Meta-Physic Supposition
Sight	Clairvoyancy
Hear	Clairaudiency
Smell	Osmosis of Incenses
Taste	Osmosis of Life Waves
Touch	Psychometrization
Thought	Telepathy
Intuition	Inspiritualization

The Ganglionic Wheels
{The Seven Vital Places of the Body}

Location	Inner Light & Sound	Function	Soul Awareness
Sahasrara	clear, white light; "thousand suns"	retainer of cosmic energy; Astral passageway; all-seeing eye	Pure Spirit
Ajna	gold in a blue field centered by brilliant white / "AUM"	third eye	Perfected Being
Vishuddha	multi-colors / "waterfalls"	ether balancer for sub-atomic spaces	Adept Being
Anahata	clear blue / tinkling bells; gongs, chimes;	vital airs of the body door to inner worlds	Free Being
Manipura	reds / flute sounds; whistling winds	physical and psychic heats; seat of 'Great Red Dragon'	Mental Plane
Svadhishthana	various, arcing whites Harp sounds	controls body fluid balances; 'two golden pipes'	Astral Plane
Muladhara	yellow; subconscious images seen in third eye / chirping sounds; grating noises	cohesion of atomic structures; base of 'kundalini (living) fire'	Material Plane

(The Sanskrit names of the vital places are from the ancient Hindu Upanishad texts)

These vital places are along the Spinal cord, also known as the 'Tree of Life', the 'Seven Astral Centers', the 'Seven Breaths', the 'Seven Spirits before the Throne', the 'Seven Temples', 'Jacob's Ladder', the path of the 'Serpentine Fire' and the 'Seven Seals'.

Note: Sahasrara; upper brain
      Ajna; between the eyebrows
      Vishuddha; base of neck
      Anahata; between the shoulders
      Manipura; behind the navel
      Svadhishthana; lower spinal cord
      Muladhara; base of spinal cord

The Correspondences of the Eleven Chakra

Location	Organ/Gland	Esoteric Response
Crown	Pineal Gland	Enlightened Existent
Forehead	Nerves	Spiritual Will
Ajna	Pituitary Gland	Spiritual Desire
Throat	Thyroid Gland	Creative Will
Front Heart	Heart	Creative Desire
Back Heart	Lungs	Gate of Wisdom
Front Solar Plexus	Stomach	Gate of Experience
Back Solar Plexus	Intestines	Gate of Mind-Reality
Spleen	Spleen	Prahna Gate
Navel	Imbilicus	Gate of Incarnation
Meng Mein	Adrenal Glands	Throne of Life Force
Sex	Sex Glands	Throne of Self-Creation
Basic	The Bones	Throne of Manifest

Influences on the Body of the Celestrial Bodies

Right-side Brain (Mercury)
Left-side Brain (Mars)
Sensory Nerves (Mercury)
Motor Nerves (Mars)
Pons Varolii (Sun)

Sympathetic Nerves (Moon)
Pineal Gland (Neptune)
Spinal Fluid (Neptune)
Spinal Cord (Moon, Mercury, Mars)

Right Eye, Heart (Sun)
Left Eye, Left Foot (Moon)
Right Nostril, Right Hand (Mars)
Mouth, Left Hand (Mercury)
Holes of the Head, Domains (Saturn)

Left Ear, Head (Jupiter)
Left Nostril, Genitals (Venus)
Right Ear, Right Foot (Saturn)

The Animation of Spirit

Path of Life Current	Description
The Earth	atmospheric world-reality; source of electro-magnetic radiance; paradise; "the rivers spring forth" the garden as Omn (om'an) and Mn (m'an)
The Feet	positive and negative poles; conduction of electro-magnetism; passage way of the soul; "souls" of the feet
The Body	host to the "wheels of light" or "urchin flowers" (chakras); shell of the astral body; Temple of consciousness; the 2 passageways (holes) of life current; place of the 4 rivers from the heart
Navel	portal of electra-radiance; channel of life substance
The Back	portal of life extinction; place of 'the wings'
The Hands	impressions of Being life force; emitters of light-radiance; encoders of consciousness
The Head	spheroid of astral light; eyes emit the light of the soul; eyes conduct the currents of life force
The Brain	converter of astral light; seed of the Being; the whole of the garden as a seed
The Aura	Being light presence; light of soul radiance

	The Holes of the Being	The Portals of the Being
The Body	Genitian passage(s), A'nu(s) passage	'soul' of the feet, 'mirrors' of hands, the 'wings', the navel
The Head	Eyes (2), Ears (2), Nose, Mouth	3rd eye, 'akasic fire' crown, 'all seeing eye

The Current of All-Knowing
(The Tree of Knowledge)

Birth (be-earth) of Consciousness

Life Force
{Qi Current}

Nervous Systems
{brain as bi-polar; body functional / sensory-motor functional}

Two Golden Pipes
{Ida and Pingala tubes of the spinal cord / flows positive & negative current}

Kulamarga Tube
{central spinal cord; Sushumna current (yellow, green electric blue)}

Wedding of Consciousness

Transformation of Astral Light
{astral sounds; 7 psychic colors}

Consumption by Astral Light
{Spistemonic (intellectual) faculty of the senses; organization of eternal realities}

Astral Light as Glory of Spirit Activity
{arrested katabolic activity of body}

Omniscient Presence
{single sense of all phenomenon; space/time disappearance; disappearance of ignorance}

Divine Ego as Pure Flame
{animation of pure spirit}

The Tree of Life

The Brain
{the golden bowl; regulator of electrical polarities: (1) cranial, (2) abdominal (reproductive center)}

The Lungs
{breath is life; purifier of poison fluid (impure blood)}

The Skin
{the veil of Individuality; transferer of sunlight-energy / renewer of vitality}

The Blood
{the river of life; absorption of glandular secretions}

The Glands
{the 'ductless'; glands that supply the bloodstream directly}

Svadhishthana and Muladhara Chakras

Gonads: 'master glands' / brain stimulus (glycogen and lactic acid); triadic relation with pituitary and pineal glands; control of entire body; source of kundalini fire

Manipura Chakra

Pancreas: "extinquisher of the fear of death"; regulates insulin, alcoholic toxins, sugars, starch; precipitates nitron gas from sunlight and atmospheric gases exposed to sunlight

Suprarenals: regulates prostrate gland, epididmis gland; makes adrenalin fluid

Vishuddha Chakra

Thyroid: exchanges body chemistry with oxygen supply

Thymus: "gland of youth" gates sexual function degeneration

Parathyroid: body functional balance; regulates calcium

Anahata Chakra

Spleen: triadic relation with pituitary, parathyroid glands; filtration of Thymus

The Tree of Life (cont.)

Ajna Chakra

Pituitary: (6th sense), regulates urine flow, milk flow, blood pressure; contracts the muscles

Speed of light reverberation, without diminishing force for thousands of years; can register or repeat any series of vibrations sent by the same instrument or with control and adjustment receive the memories of others; vibrations are mathematically calculable to speeds of varying degrees corresponding to the speed of light squared.

In negative state (receptive phase), gives knowledge by repeating impulses of the 5 other vital centers.

Sahasrara Chakra

Pineal: the Buddhi; the Conarium; all seeing eye

Direct contact with cosmic vibration; channel of intuition; super-sensory wisdom; conductor of psychic auras; seat of psychic faculties; knowledge of past and future; memory, expectancy, anticipatancy; enabler of the manipulation and vibrational uses of the 6th sense; enabler to attract free atoms to reproduce the forms of any manifest of atomic phenomenon.

The Manifest of Individuality

Core: { **The Soul Essence**
{ Substance of Spirit Attraction; Adamic Dust / Evian Mist

The Five Coverings of the Soul

The First Covering: { **The Electra Cell**
{ The Ego; Senses Separation, Discrimination, Feeling and Creative Medium

The Second Covering: { **The Magnetic Aura**
{ Field of Life Forces and Attraction of Cosmic Radiation

The Third Covering: { **The Mental Cloud**
{ Reservoir of Cosmic Electricity and Intelligible Spaces

The Fourth Covering: { **The Astral Body**
{ The Vehicle Body of Cosmic Absorption; The LifeGhost

The Fifth Covering: { **The Physical Body**
{ The Vehicle Body of Cosmic Impression(s)

Being Who Is, I Am That, I Am

                  Light of Divine Power
Light of Intelligence   {Divine Love}   Light of Sacred Vibration

{Realm of Divine Spirit _____

                {Path of the Light of Life}
                Divine Creative Consciousness
Divine Magnetism   Divine Intelligence   Divine Act   Divine Light

                    Divine Being
Divine Nature   Divine Consciousness   Divine Energy   Divine Radiance

{Realm of the Word _____

                    Divine Image
                {Light-rays of Angelic Being(s)}

                 {Body of Vital Currents}
          Attracting / Crystallizing / Metabolizing
        Assimilating / Circulating / Eliminating / Repelling

                  Divine Manifest
                 {World of Darkness}

{World of Aura-Electriciti(es)_____**World** of Aura-Magnetism**}**

          {Dual Polarity Field(s) of World Realit(ies)}
      Positive   Neutralizing   Negative

{Causual Soul Body _____

     Ego   Feeling   Discrimination   Mind-Intellect

{Life Body _____

   Physical Senses   Physical Action   Mental Attraction

  ether/gas/liquid/fire/substance   events / impressions   cause(s)-effect(s)

Word-sounds of the Seven Planets
(from alpha beta spoken symbols)

Mercury {me cur i}, {me cur i(s)}, {mec(a) ur is(is)}, {m' ecuris}

Venus {ve nu (s)}, {ve nu is(is)}, {venu is}, {venu is(is)}, {v'nu is}, {v'nu is(is)}

Urantia {ur an(a)t}, {ur r(a) anat}, {an(u) at}, {anat}, {(ur)'e ra}, *{ur't}

Mars {mar s'}, { m' aris}, {m' ars}, {m'ar s'}, {m' ar(i)s(is)}, {m(a) r(a) (is)is}

Jupiter {ju pi ter(re)}, {ju piter}, {ju pi t(i) r(a)}, {j'up piter}, {j' u pi terra}

Saturn {s' at urn}, {s' at ur n}, {(i)s' at urn}, {s' atu r(a) n(u)}, {s' atu ur ra nu}

Uranus {ur anus}, {ur anu (i)s}, {ur r(a) nu (s)}, {ur r(a) nu is}, {ur r(a) nu is(is)}

Table of De-coded Numerology

1 2 3 4 5 6 7 8 9   {1+2+3+4+5+6+7+8+9=46 or: 10}

5 8   2 9   3 6   {58+29+36=123 or: 6}

---

1   4   7   {1+4+7= 12 or: 3}

---

1 2   {1+2=3 or: 3}

---

3 :   {3(sq.) , 9(cu.) , etc.}

Alternating series: { 1, 3, 5, 7, 9 } or: { 1 + 3 + 5 + 7 + 9 = 25 } or: { 2 + 5 = 7 }

1 2 3 4 5 6 7 8 9	9 x 1 = 9/9 or: 9 / 9 = 9
2 3 4 5 6 7 8 9	9 x 2 = 1'8 or: 1 + 8 = 9
3 4 5 6 7 8 9	9 x 3 = 2'7 or: 2 + 7 = 9
4 5 6 7 8 9	9 x 4 = 3'6 or: 3 + 6 = 9
5 6 7 8 9	9 x 5 = 4'5 or: 4 + 5 = 9
6 7 8 9 (beginning retrograde motional awareness.........	9 x 6 = 5'4 or: 5 + 4 = 9
7 8 9	9 x 7 = 6'3 or: 6 +3 = 9
8 9	9 x 8 = 7'2 or: 7 + 2 = 9
9 (continued infinitum)..........	9 x 9 = 8'1 or: 8 + 1 = 9

Triadic Correspondences of Twelve (Western) Musical Keys

C ma { F ma, G ma }
Saturn Periodic / (+) / Aries/ (cardinal) / Fire / Crown, Head, / red, red-orange
    Aries: (Virgo, Scorpio)

B b ma { E b ma, F ma }
Vital Body (+) / Aquarius (fixed) /Air / Legs / blue, aqua-marine
    Aquarius: (Cancer, Virgo)

A b ma { D b ma, E b ma }
Mind Desire Spirit / (+) / Sagittarius (mutable) / Fire / Lower Torso, Upper Thigh / green
    Sagittarius: (Taurus, Cancer)

F # ma { B ma, C # ma }
Spirit-Individuality (+) / Libra (cardinal) / Air / Lower Back, Buttocks, Skin / orange
    Libra: (Pisces, Taurus)

E b ma { A b ma, B b ma }
Life Spirit / (-) / Cancer (cardinal) / Water / Navel, Womb / blue-green
    Cancer: (Sagittarius, Aquarius)

D b ma { G b ma, A b ma }
Saturn Periodic / (-) / Taurus (fixed) / Earth / Throat, Neck, Shoulders / orange-yellow
    Taurus: (Libra, Sagittarius)

B ma { E b ma, F ma }
Dense Body / (-) / Pisces (mutable) / Water / Feet, Ankles / violet
    Pisces: (Cancer, Virgo)

A ma { D ma, E ma }
Vital Body / (-) / Capricorn (cardinal) / Earth / Knees, Skin / green-blue
    Capricorn: (Gemini, Leo)

G ma { C ma, D ma }
Mental Desire Body / (-) / Scorpio (fixed) / Water / Genitals, Nose / yellow
    Scorpio: (Aries, Gemini)

F ma { B b ma, C ma }
Divine Life Spirit / (-) / Virgo (mutable) / Stomach, Abdomen / yellow-green
    Virgo: (Aquarius, Aries)

Triadic Correpondences (Continued)

E ma { A ma, B ma }
Divine Spiritual Will / (+) / Leo / Fire (fixed) / Heart, Visage, Spine / gold, indigo
    Leo: (Capricorn, Pisces)   { Saturn Periodic / Flame }

D ma { G ma, A ma }
Human Spirit / (+) / Gemini (mutable) / Air / Hands, Arms, Lungs / blue-yellow
    Gemini: (Scorpio, Capricorn)

Atlantian Correspondences to Sound and the Seven Colors

<u>Red</u> corresponding to <u>F sharp</u> (major)

<u>Orange</u> corresponding to <u>B flat</u> (major)

<u>Gold</u> corresponding to <u>G</u> (major)

<u>Green</u> corresponding to <u>C</u> and <u>E</u> in combination (major)

<u>Blue</u> corresponding to <u>E flat</u> (major)

<u>Indigo</u> corresponding to <u>A</u> (minor)

<u>Violet</u> corresponding to <u>B, D, G</u> in triadic combination (major)

Study Cycle Based Upon the Twelve Celestrial Personalities

Cycle 1: (Aries)   New Concepts / New Approaches / New Lessons

Cycle 2: (Taurus)   Exercises / Sequence Studies / Technique Studies

Cycle 3: (Gemini)   Interpret / Rehearse / Observe Relationships

Cycle 4: (Cancer)   Melodic Studies / Rhythm Studies / Compose

Cycle 5: (Leo)   Test Strengths / Eccentricity

Cycle 6: (Virgo)   Read / Research / Formulate

Cycle 7: (Libra)   Classes / Balance Activities / Integrate Researches

Cycle 8: (Scorpio)   Criticize / Correct

Cycle 9: (Sagittarius) Adjustments / Explore Potentials

Cycle 10: (Capricorn) Review / Organize

Cycle 11: (Aquarius) Experiment / Test Ideas / Apply New Concepts

Cycle 12: (Pisces)   Express from the Heart / Allow the Spirit Intervention

Seven Attributes of the Initiate

The Power of Magnitude

The ability to be of cosmic consciousness in awareness of All That Is. The internalized revelation of being as Spirit working through the manifested body.

The Power of Minuteness

The ability to see into the smallest particles of matter, the insight into the inter-workings of force, time, space and light-energy. The ability to see into the hearts of living creatures.

The Power of Spirit/Body Separation

The ability to recognize the inertial force(s) of nature. The ability to recognize the sub-conscious will as the host to manifesting destiny, eradicating karma and for the belonging into the world as "of the world but not in it".

The Power of Irresistible Will

The ability to recognize the true nature of things as being unstable, temporary and subject to change. Knowing this the initiate can pass through any obstacle.

The Power of Attainment

The ability to manipulate the power of magnetic attraction. The ability to attain any desire by the application of creative visualization, and so, adjusting the world circumstances around the being.

The Power of Lightness

The ability to express Divine Creative power without restriction, giving reality to the Divine Spiritual existence. The ability to create whole universes.

The Power of God-Conscious

The ability to exist in the perpetual revelation of the Divine Will. The ability to "overcome the world".

Fifteen Attributes of the Mystic-Experiant

The Power to Know the Thoughts of Other Beings
{Telepathiac}

The Power to Control the Circumstances of Events
{Cosmi-radiatraic}

The Power to Manipulate the Forces of Nature
{Cosmi-electriatic}

The Power to Transform Matter by Thought
{Psycho-kinetriac}

The Power to Transform Perceptions of Immediate Realiti(es)
{Psycho-Intrinsciac}

The Power to Channel Spirits
{Mediumity}

The Power to Appear as a Spirit of Another Being
{Aura-magnetiac}

The Power to Spiritually Appear within the Body of Another Being
{Corpor-magnetiac}

The Power to Pro-create without Sexual Intercourse
{Parthenogeni-radiatriaic}

The Power to See into the Akashic Records
{Control of Destiny}

The Power to Astral Project at Will
{Spirit-trajectoriac)

The Power to Command Events by Word
{Auto-prahnaic}

The Power to Manipulate Atomic Structures by Sound
{Atomo-auralaic}

The Power to Commune with Spirit Essences
{Pure-spirit Consciousness}

The Power to Directly Recognize and Know the Omni-Presence of Divine Intelligence
{God Consciousness}

Meditation

The purpose of meditation is to still the mind for to allow for the vital forces of cosmic illumination to enter into one's spiritual conscious so to experience the wonder of enlightenment.

Meditation in practice will sooth the mind, correct problems of health and by the power of the will of it, also effects the immediate environment(s). As a result from the frequency of meditation, the initiate will discover the ability to create mental waves that may become powerful enough for to attain dominion over all things.

The initiate gains an advantage to control destiny by meditating upon any thought or desire. By the uses of both focused concentration and by creative visualization, it should be instantly accepted that no inspiritualized projected thought goes unrealized or not manifested in the real-existent world.

As a rule, personal prayers are best kept in secret, while prayers for others may be shared in compassionate love. By practicing so, there will be achieved a balance of psychic energy without depletion. Psychic energy is important to control for assuring the development and retention of spiritual power.

Ultimately, it is most desirable that the meditation focus simply on the workings of Creation, which is accomplished quite readily by allowing the spirit to commune, without personal inclinations of thought, directly into the cosmic field of the Astral Light, thereby accepting Divine Intelligence.

Because Intelligence begets Intelligence, it is encouraged that the meditation session always ends by an acknowledgement that there is no separation between being-entities and that of the Divine. It is for this reason that an appreciation for the mystic correspondence be demonstrated. At first, it is a personal experience, and appreciation may be demonstrated as a personal gesture. As faith in the demonstrations accumulates with experiences, human nature begins to cause one to overtly express one's strength of faith to others. While this may encourage some, it should be recognized that the demonstrations from meditation remain reflective of one's own spiritual development, and that another's level of development may be either higher or beneath one's own. Therefore, the most effective outward praise should be that as a continued demonstration of the meditation discipline. Those who know the same experience will be joined unto it as a matter of spiritual accord.

It remains, however, vital that the initiate continues to find ways that will encourage others to enter into an expedient path for their enlightenment.

The Prahnic Voice: Sound-Word Power (Invocation)

Within the breath is carried the prahnic current of creation. The initiate realizes the wonder-sound of creation by the invocation of sound-words of power as the vehicle to the invisible worlds. It is sound as word transforming the yearnings of the heart into reality-existence. This is the act of the vibrationist.

The practices of invocation are forms of prayer that make use of spiritual desire, visualization, breath, word-sound and the word-intent. While the invocations of words 'from the passionate heart' will always be of spiritual innocence, the mystic masters throughout the ages have habitually left invocations with which to pass down exacting expressions of precisely ordered cosmic alignments, thereby revealing entrance ways of spiritual transcendentalism.

Make no mistake, regardless of the exacting 'scientific' approach to prayer by precise invocations, the most important aspect of its success is rooted in the degree of love for the experience. However, knowing that attaining great love is an act that needs to be cultivated as part of the spiritual development, the mystic masters have devised ways wherein an assured path of discovery may be offered to their relating masses.

Invocations have been practiced in the form of mantras, chants, by reading aloud from sacred writings or by being possessed directly of Holy Ghost, which offers 'speaking in tongues' or imitating any sound. All of these forms of invocation are channel-means to inspire the move of Spirit. It is also a means by which initiates can simultaneously share in the experience.

The sound of 'aum' is heard while in deep meditation. 'Aum', then, may be experienced by anyone regardless of any devotional grouping. (Aum is also approximated as 'Amn' or 'Amen').

Word-sounds existing in this world can be of more or of less profound power and effect. Many are cultural attachments that do not necessarily attempt to reach the universality of the world's beings. Others are no longer as effective, due to changed reality-existences. The initiate may discover by comparison the powers and the effects of various invocations.

Invocation will immediately effect the reality atmospheres. It is, yet, another bringing from the music of the spheres.

Awareness of the Current Force of Pulse-Intelligence

Throughout the ages, the mystic masters have recognized that the Cosmic Pulse-Intelligence currents its force within all phenomena and that its flow patterns can be mapped to vital node points of the physical manifest. From the moles on our bodies to the stars in the heavens, these vital node points are realized to all creatures, in all of nature.

The vital node points are the places of wonder manifest of magnificent beauty and God-presence. This is where we find refuge for the Spirit. They are the places of magnetic intensity. Most often, we respect such places as being sacred. They are at the wellsprings of the waters, the hollows of the earth, the places of the winds, or at the places that let light-radiance.

It is through the portals of these vital node points that the energy of the universe lets itself in currents of its force. To direct the force from where it is apparent offers the attainment of power to heal illness, to prolong life, and to correct all disorders of human error.

In particular to us as human beings, the careful study of vital node points of and about the body has resulted in certain science practices of the healing arts. Acupuncture, Qi Gong, Shiatsu, Tai Chi and Falun Gong are all highly evolved arts of ancient origin. These arts represent the practices of 'laying on of the hands' and of the developed personal command over one's own life force.

The advanced martial arts also teach the use of releasing one's 'chi' energy through the palms and fingertips, the soles of the feet, and even through the eyes and with the sound power of the voice.

Brought together by these practices is the knowledge of the science scholar and the intuition of the mystical initiate.

Through these two attributes of the personality, we are able to discover still more profound truths about our existence.

It becomes essential, then, that the initiate should recognize one's own 'chi' energy flow patterns and how it reinforces the power of the creative potential.

The Ideas of Spiritual Contemplation

The Light of the Creator lets the Blessings of Revelation.

The Universe is immersed in sacredness.

All phenomena are subject to the impression of Intelligence.

The pulse of Intelligence currents each thing in Life with its own life-force.

The Deities exist within the Invisible World.

The World of the Deities, the World of Nature and the World of Human Beings are unbroken continua, with each world being distinct yet inseparable to All.

The Deities of the Invisible World are the spirit-ascended humans of yesterday and the humans of today are destined to become the Deities of tomorrow.

The presence of the Deities recorded in Earthly history were for to make known the love-knowledge that will inspiritualize humanity.

Ingress into the Minds of the Deities can be attained through intuition.

All phenomena are subject to the laws of Cause and Effect.

The World of Causes exists within the Invisible World, the true World of Reality, is invisible to the eyes of the flesh but not to the eyes of the spirit.

The various Act(s) of the soul personality are the expression of the soul's inspiritualization, the soul's spiritual maturity and of the soul's age.

The human practices of ritual are the acts of acknowledgement to the realiti(es) of the world(s) of Earthly-Spiritual Duality and of Divine Cause(s).

The Visible World lets the World of Effects.

Divine Order rents all mystic phenomena from Chaos.

The conscious Acts of Cause(s) within the World of Effects is the Experience of Life.

✷ ✷ ✷ ✷ ✷ ✷ ✷

...they shall behold this Son of woman sitting upon the throne of his glory.
(LXI-9)

Then shall the kings, the princes, and all who possess the earth, glorify him who has dominion over all things, him who was concealed; for from the beginning the Son of man existed in secret, whom the Most High preserved in the presence of his power, and revealed to the elect.
(LXI-10)

...Before the sun and the signs were created, before the stars of heaven were formed, his name was invoked in the presence of the Lord of spirits.
(XLIII-3)

– The Book of Enoch, The Prophet

"As above, so below..."

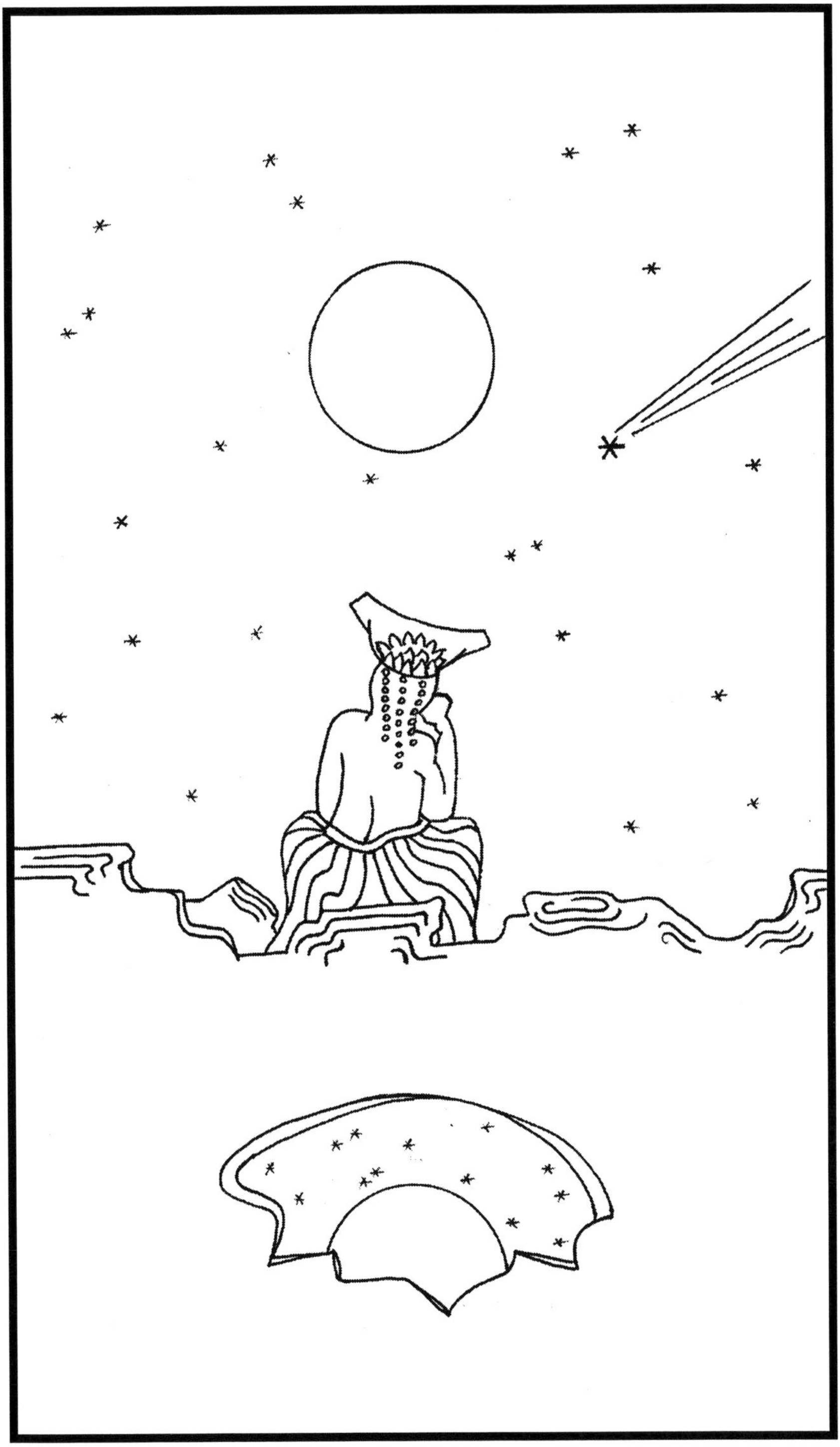

To Order Books, E-Books, CDs or Art Prints
please visit the website address:
www.djukemusic.com

For a complete catalog listing, or to become more aware about the author, please visit the website.

All art drawings are available in printed display formats ©2004.

On Mu Music Press
New York

To Order

Please send me _____ printed copie(s) of EXERCIRICLE:

Name: _____

Mailing Address: _____

City, State, Code: _____

Country: _____

E-Mail Address: _____

Telecommunication (optional): _____

Each printed copy of EXERCIRICLE sells for $20.00 U.S.
Please add $5.00 U.S. for shipping & handling.

Total Amount Enclosed: _____

Send to: On Mu Music Press
          209 E. 7th St., Suite 3W
          New York, NY 10009

Please send cash, money order or cashier's check ONLY!
For credit card transactions, please order through the website:
www.djukemusic.com

(You may photocopy this Order Form to preserve this page of your book.)